FRITZ

the Cinema Cat
Gets His Wings

written by *Louise Adela Nye*

illustrated by *Jo Lundstrom Smith*

Order this book online at www.trafford.com/07-2274
or email orders@trafford.com

Most Trafford titles are also available at major online book retailers.

Map Illustration on Page 95 by Sam Miles
Back Cover Photo by Cathie Newman

Note for Librarians: A cataloguing record for this book is available from Library
and Archives Canada at www.collectionscanada.ca/amicus/index-e.html

Printed in Victoria, BC, Canada.

ISBN: 978-1-4251-5193-5

*We at Trafford believe that it is the responsibility of us all, as both individuals
and corporations, to make choices that are environmentally and socially sound.
You, in turn, are supporting this responsible conduct each time you purchase a
Trafford book, or make use of our publishing services. To find out how you are
helping, please visit www.trafford.com/responsiblepublishing.html*

*Our mission is to efficiently provide the world's finest, most comprehensive
book publishing service, enabling every author to experience success.
To find out how to publish your book, your way, and have it available
worldwide, visit us online at www.trafford.com/10510*

www.trafford.com

North America & international
toll-free: 1 888 232 4444 (USA & Canada)
phone: 250 383 6864 ♦ fax: 250 383 6804
email: info@trafford.com

The United Kingdom & Europe
phone: +44 (0)1865 487 395   local rate: 0845 230 9601
facsimile: +44 (0)1865 481 507   mail: info.uk@trafford.com

10 9 8 7 6 5 4

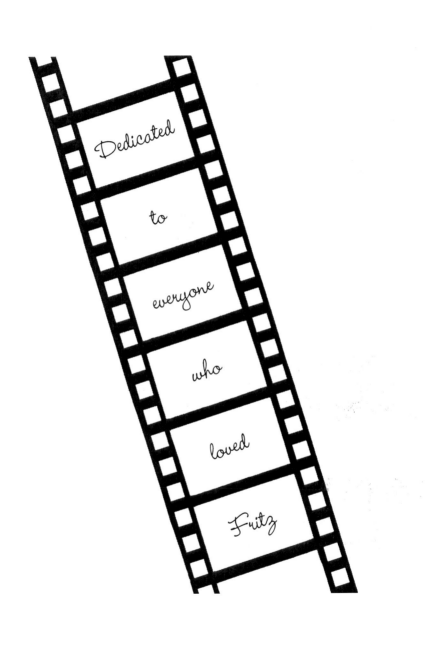

On a special island called Salt Spring, there's a movie theatre in an old community hall. It has a covered front porch, and on that porch there once was a little house. That's where I used to live, but not anymore. The house is gone and so am I.

If you'd like to find out where I went, then sit back, get comfy, and I will tell you about my most wonderful adventure yet.

Early one evening in February, something happened that changed my life forever. That day began in the usual way. My guardian delivered my food and water, like she did every morning.

She also talked to me, gave me lots of pats, and a good brushing. While I was munching away, I wondered how many other cats got all that attention, as well as nibbles-on-wheels.

After I finished eating, I jumped up on my phone booth tower to watch the traffic go by. People called out "Hi Fritz!" and waved to me on their way to work and school.

A while later, I scampered across the parking lot to the long grass at the edge, where I liked to hide and explore.

Then I went behind the hall to my big backyard. It's really a cemetery, where people come to look at certain stones and put flowers beside them.

While I was wandering around, a man arrived. He stood looking at one of the stones for quite a while, then he put down a single pink rose.

Before he left, he said, "Watch over her for me, Fritz. That's a good cat."

I wished that I could talk, so I could ask him to explain what he meant.

I spent the afternoon poking about in the woods nearby, then settled down for a long catnap. When I woke up I was hungry and thirsty, so I made my way back to the porch. I wondered what was on that evening at the hall. Since I had seen the film canisters taken away earlier in a van, I knew there wouldn't be a movie that night, so it had to be the dog-training class. I always enjoyed those.

The dogs wouldn't be arriving with their owners until almost dark. I would have quite a long wait, so I thought I'd like to go somewhere.

Maybe I'd get a juicy snack at one of the houses next door, or I could go to the flying-ball place, the golf course. I liked the way the short grass felt under my paws, like a thick, plush carpet.

I finally decided to go over to the fire hall where I'd probably have some company. I made sure there was no traffic, then I crossed the road.

The fire fighters always made me feel welcome as they checked the hoses, cleaned the equipment and polished the chrome on the big red fire trucks.

I stayed until it started to get dark. There was a chill in the air and in my bones. It was time to go back to my cozy little house on the porch. I stretched my legs and waited for a gap in the traffic. Then, taking a deep breath I darted for the other side... at that moment, my day suddenly stopped being an ordinary one, as

WHAM!!!

I was hit

by

a

passing

car...

Struggling to make it back to the steps of the porch, I crawled underneath. I panted desperately and found it difficult to catch my breath. I heard ladies' voices, was picked up and gently placed into a car that took off up the road.

I knew it wasn't another catnapping, as I heard the driver say, "Please hang on Fritz. We'll soon be at the vet's."

I did my best to stay awake but I became so weak that I felt I just had to close my eyes. Then, the strangest thing happened! I floated straight out of the roof of the car! I popped down again and saw a white cat on the seat, looking ever so quiet and still.

With a start, I realized that the cat down there was me! How can I be up here and awake, yet at the same time, lying down there with my eyes shut?

We soon arrived at the vet's and I watched as I was carefully taken inside.

He examined me, turned to the upset lady and slowly shook his head. He made a phone call, and after a while, my food-delivery lady arrived, looking so sad. I wondered what would happen next.

Suddenly, a small Siamese cat appeared. She stared at me with almond-shaped blue eyes and said, "It's all right, Fritz, I'm here to help you."

"Who are YOU ? How do you know my name? What makes you think I need help? And by the way, are you on your way to a costume party, or are those wings real?"

"My name is Misty. Everyone on the island knows who you are and yes, the wings are really mine. Are you sure you're all right?"

"I'll be okay once I wake up. Boy this is the craziest dream I've ever had!"

"It's no dream, Fritz. It's really happening!"

"Then I'd rather be somewhere else, but how do I get there?"

"You just have to think of a place and you'll be there, Fritz, it's as simple as that."

You mean I can just beam myself anywhere? As much as I'd like to do that outer-space stuff, I think I'd just as soon go home."

As quick as the flick of a mouse's tail, there we were on the front porch of the hall. It worked, just like she said it would. It was amazing!

Then I remembered that the dog-training class was going on and I didn't want to miss it.

"Follow me, Misty, this will be a real blast!"

We walked through the front door of the hall, even though it was closed!

"Whoa, how did we do that?"

We jumped on the backs of the cinema seats that had been pushed against the walls.

The dogs paraded around the hall with their owners while we watched.

Every time they passed by us, I'd swish my bushy tail, wave my paws and tease them something awful. Sometimes they'd glance over our way, but mostly, they ignored us. Could it have been that they just didn't see me?

"This is totally boring, Misty. Let's go back outside." I showed her my house and while I was talking about my tower, we ended up on top of it! "Whoops, how did THAT happen?"

"Okay, Fritz, think about it. You can walk through closed doors and you seem to be invisible, right? Also, you don't hurt even though you were hit by a car. Why do you suppose that is?"

"Let me see. It could be that I've got these special powers because I've turned into a SUPERCAT. Yeah, that's it!"

Misty laughed and said, "You've been watching too many movies, Fritz."

"Well, I have seen quite a few, especially those zany animated ones."

"Then you know that cartoon characters always keep bouncing back for more, as you said in your book, Fritz. But they're not real, are they?"

Misty was right again. What a smart cat she was! I thought for a while, then I finally got it. "Misty, could it be that I've, died? And if so, WHY? Why ME? Why NOW?"

"Your time was up, that's all."

"That's ALL? You mention it like it's only a bent whisker or a burr in my tail, but it's no small thing!"

"**Y**ou're right, Fritz. Other than being born, it's probably the most important thing that's ever happened to you. The wonder of it is, that even though you're no longer in your body, another part of you, your spirit, lives forever and ever."

"Wow! Does everyone know this Misty?"

"No, but they will when it's their turn, and won't they be surprised!"

"They sure will..... So what happens now, Misty?"

"Well there's a special place that's called by many different names. Some of them are: the Other Side... the Great Beyond... the Hereafter... the Promised Land... Eternity... Paradise... and even the Happy Hunting Grounds.

But I like to call it Heaven. That's where you'll go when you leave here."

"Leave HERE? Why would I want to do that? This is my home, and my friends are here. I couldn't leave them, my little house, or the cinema. NEVER!" After I calmed down, I asked her, "What's it like in the place with many names, this Heaven, and where it is anyway?"

"It's more wonderful than you could ever imagine, Fritz, and it's not far away at all. It's just in another dimension. Also, you can come back and visit any time you want."

"Another dimension? You've got to be kidding! You mean I'd be changing my size, and get huge like a floating balloon cat in a parade, or shrink down to be small like a wind-up toy? I don't think so! I happen to like myself just the way I am. And I want to stay here ALL the time, not just visit now and then like a tourist."

"Well, you think about it, Fritz."

And with that Misty disappeared. I wondered how she knew so much. Maybe there's a school for cats in Heaven...

That was a very long night. When morning came, I sat up on my tower but nobody waved as they passed by. I was feeling quite lonely, then Misty came back.

"How would you like to go on a tour of the island, Fritz?"

"Sure, but no more talk about going to that Heaven place, okay?"

Misty agreed, so off we went to places that I thought I'd never get to see! It was like a magical mystery tour on a flying carpet! First, we darted in and out of little fairy doors in the big trees on Mount Erskine.

"Where are the fairies Misty?"

"Since they're so shy, Fritz, they must be hiding."

We did see a carved stone water dish with a plaque on it. It was in memory of Rosie, a three-legged dog that used to walk the trails. Then, off we went to see another kind of ferry in the South end.

We leapt on the cars and trucks in the lineup, then onto the Fulford Ferry. When the loud hoot blasted, it startled us. We jumped, then laughed ourselves silly as we rolled over the waves in the harbour.

In the village, we buzzed about little shops and studios, seeing all sorts of cool things: fun toys, way-out sculptures, hats galore, and trillions of teensy beads.

Along a sideroad, we zoomed through a school, and more studios.

Then we went to Fulford Hall. "Look at those painted banners fluttering down there from the ceiling, Misty! But there doesn't seem to be a movie screen anywhere."

We also checked out the hall at Beaver Point that had a really tall fireplace. "There's no screen either, Misty, and I wonder where the beavers are? Maybe they are hiding."

The people of the island, we discovered, live in many different kinds of houses. There are rammed-earths, straw-bale, undergrounds, domes, yurts, trailers, tents and tree-houses!

There were mansions with decks that dangled on cliffs over the ocean, tiny cabins in the woods, new condos in town and funky houseboats on the water.

In a big valley we saw little churches, large farms, and many sheep, horses, goats, chickens, llamas, alpacas, quite a few dogs and lots of cats.

We also discovered sprawling vineyards, another golf course and a big old farm that has a school and a yoga centre.

On the top of Mount Maxwell we perched in the twiggy nest of a heron and gazed out over the dark blue ocean to

other islands

far away...

Then, in the village of Ganges, we had fun zooming through places that cats rarely go. We saw more schools, and one had fancy painted fish swirling along its fence.

The big theatre called Artspring had lots of way-out art on the walls, a miniature sailing ship in a big glass case and comfy-looking seats that overlooked a stage. The ceiling had coloured lights and there was a booth with many complicated switches.

We also went to Mahon Hall and it had a stage and fancy lights, but no screen that I could see. So, I figured that my Central Hall was the only place for showing movies on the island!

There was, however, a fantastic store downtown that had hundreds of videos for people to take home and watch on their TV's. There was even free popcorn, so the owners must really be nice people.

Farther on down the street, we were excited to discover bubbles floating out from the roof of a soap shop. We had fun chasing them around and popping them with our paws and whiskers.

Islanders sure must read a lot, as we found a library and about six book shops in Ganges. One even had my picture on the front door!

Next, we went to the marinas, and oh the boats we saw! Sailboats, motor boats, fishing boats, rowboats, kayaks, tour boats and even seaplanes!

We saw a big black and white cat jump from his home on a trimaran into a rowboat. He looked over at us with great curiosity, so I think he saw us. When it docked, a tall man got out and the cat ran off to explore. I'll bet he'd have some stories to tell!

Sitting under the big gazebo in Centennial Park, Misty asked me if there was anywhere else that I'd like to go.

"I'd like to go to Vesuvius, Misty."

"Do you mean in far off Italy?"

"Have you been watching the Travel Channel, Misty? No, it's right here on the island. Come on!"

In Vesuvius we saw a community of little houses near a really great beach that had lots of shells and driftwood. There was also a ferry terminal, a tiny general store, many interesting studios and a restaurant that overlooked the bay.

We then zoomed up to the north end and spotted a unique wall mural on the outside of a school. We ended our tour at Southey Point, as waves crashed in over the rocks.

Our island was even more spectacular than I'd realized. How could I ever leave it all behind?

Back at the porch, a huge surprise was waiting for me. Pots of colourful flowers were sitting beside my house, and even on my roof! There were cards, a new cat dish and other gifts, too, and they kept arriving all that day and into the evening.

However, when people dropped them off, they didn't even stay to pat me or talk, even though I was right there. That wasn't like our friendly island people at all!

Later that night, the square-dancers arrived. I joined them on the old wooden floor and twirled around like I usually did, but nobody paid any attention to me.

The next evening was movie night, my favourite time. I spotted the popcorn girl and walked up the aisle toward her. She looked straight at me with a surprised look on her face. She could see me, I knew it! But then, she looked away and went into the kitchen, where I heard her softly crying.

I went back to the lobby to settle down on my favourite chair, but my cushion was missing! I sat there and waited for people to come and say hello, but they only glanced my way! They talked quietly to each other and looked ever so sad.

I went outside, where I saw the lady in the black hat, who was tacking up a photo of me on my house.

She whispered, "Are you there, Fritz?" I think she knew I was beside her, but she just couldn't see me. I guess I really must be invisible!

When I heard the movie start, I went back inside and jumped up on some laps but I got no pats at all.

I was happy when the owner sat down on a seat near the stairs to the booth.

I leapt on his lap and thought that if I sat there long enough, I'd become visible to him and he would talk to me and give me some pats.

But, that didn't happen. Somehow, I knew that he was thinking about me, though, and that made me feel a lot better.

In a few days, it was the painters' turn to use the hall. I used to go around to each artist and look at their paintings, and I would get smiles, pats and kind words. This time, I wasn't even noticed!

Days went by, and people brought even more presents and pots of flowers. There was even one on my tower!

A man came by and took pictures. I heard later on that there were some in our local paper, and write-ups about me, too. It took me back to the time when I was catnapped. I've sure caused a lot of "Fritz frenzies" on the island!

SALT SPRING CINEMA

OSCAR AWARD
FOR BEST CAT
FRITZ

FRITZ THE CAT

Remembering Fritz

Let's Remember Fritz

Fritz takes final bow

"I bet he had more friends than anybody on the Island."
— Cathie Newman

By SEAN McINTYRE
Driftwood Staff

Michael Levy still finds it hard to believe Fritz the Cinema Cat isn't there when he shows up for work at Central Hall each afternoon.

"Normally I would open the door and he'd be waiting," said The Fritz owner-operator last weekend. "Now you open the door and he's nowhere to be found. It feels very strange."

Animal lover Cathie Newman still finds herself in the habit of stopping by the hall some mornings after years of caring for the cinema cat.

"He was my little bit of sunshine," Newman said. "I bet he had more friends than anybody on the island."

When Fritz arrived at Central Hall from his letterboard home on Fort Street near Walker Hook, he bore little resemblance to the cat so many island residents have come to know and love.

Life was tough up north and Fritz eventually decided he'd had enough and began his great southbound trek, only to end up at the centre of an island's attentions.

Within weeks, community members donated a flea scratching post, a makeshift shelter and small bedding, and Central Hall's board of directors warmed to the idea of having a resident cat.

"Part of what made him an integral member of the cinema was that it took some time to develop this relationship," Levy said. "At first, it was just that there was this cat hanging out and it kept hanging out and that sort of started a whole chain of events. He just showed up, and developed this relationship with everybody. After all was said and done and people got used to him, he got used to people."

Levy earned the cinema in the cat's honour when he purchased the business in September 2004. His devotion stemmed more from a desire to express the Fritz spirit rather than using Prizz as a gimmick to publicize the theatre.

"It was never a ploy or thing where you ring a bell and expect him to show up," he said.

"This is a defining part of who we are. Fritz showed that we can come together even though we don't always agree."

"We do have this spirit and we are not Vancouver, Victoria, Nanaimo or Duncan. We are Salt Spring Island and there are a lot of unique features here."

Fritz achieved off-island fame in August 2005 when a Richmond animal rights activist attempted to save the feline from what she deemed the cinema's unsympathetic use of the animal to sell movie tickets and concerns for his welfare. News of the cat-napping staggered an island-wide search and Fritz was eventually returned.

Levy said he still cannot believe the community's response to the event.

FLOWERS FOR FRITZ: Cinema owner Michael Levy pauses near a bouquet left in one of Fritz's favourite haunts.

as a gimmick to publicize the theatre.

"This is a little animal and people were willing to pitch in for him. You can only imagine what would have happened if a small child was taken," he said.

"Salt Spring came together to fight for an animal that had no means of fighting for itself when somebody came along and grabbed him."

Louise Nye, author of the recently published Fritz the Cinema Cat, couldn't help but feel inspired by the feline's tale.

Fritz, she said, proved how precise could always be found close to home and showed the great isn't always greener on the other side of the fence.

"He showed us that something good can come from tragedy," she said.

Nye is planning to write a sequel titled Fritz and his Afterlife.

"I want to show that life can continue, that there is not an absolute end," she added.

Not only has the news of Fritz's passing left a sense of emptiness among those who cared for him, but many island residents are wondering if life will ever be the same at Central Hall.

"He was so much to so many people," Levy said. "The response has been incredible. Some people just stopped seeing him as their way to and from work."

Just before 5 p.m. on Wednesday, February 21, Fritz, aged 11, wandered into the path of an oncoming vehicle in front of the theatre. Reasons for the incident remain unclear, although some accounts report Fritz was "spooked" off the Central Hall steps.

Fritz was dead by the time he arrived at veterinarian Malcolm Bond's office.

"He bled out internally and was dead on arrival," said Bond.

Well-wishers began placing flowers and notes in front of Fritz's resting spot outside the hall. Over the weekend, a small plant appeared atop the telephone booth Fritz used to catch the late-afternoon sun.

Judging by the community's response, the island isn't likely to hear the end of Fritz for some time.

The driving behind the wheel of the vehicle has offered to lend her creative talent to the sculpting of a commemorative statue and Levy would like to install a plaque just above Fritz's home.

Central Hall Society chair David Mink said Fritz's ingenious hopefully translate into some long-awaited action to improve traffic safety at the Central intersection.

"We are all quite devastated," he said.

"If anything, this might be the impetus for something positive at that intersection. How hard can it be to put up two more stop signs?"

Organizers are planning what they hope will rank among the island's largest memorial services when the citizens doors are opened for parties to bid Fritz a final salute on March 10.

Humourist Arthur Black will host the event at 2 p.m. and Salt Spring musician Jamie RT will perform a special number in the cat's memory.

"It's time for Salt Springers to get together and remember one of their own. I hope we can really celebrate Fritz's spirit," Levy said.

"He defined what it is to be a good community."

Plans to replace Fritz with a theatre cat from Prince George remain premature, Levy added.

While arrangements are underway to rescue Dave the cat, Levy added, there is not guarantee he will make up residence as the Fritz Cinema.

"I don't think it's the right time," he said.

"We'll have to wait and see what happens."

Proceeds from this ad will be donated to the SPCA.

Gulf Islands
Drift-wood

I was happy to see Misty one morning and I said to her, "No, I haven't changed my mind. I'm still not leaving, not now or ever, not even to get a pair of super-great wings, like you have!"

"Don't get your tail in a twist, Fritz, I just stopped by to see how you were."

I must have looked like I needed cheering up, as Misty asked, "Are you up for another trip? How would you like to see where I used to live?"

That sounded good to me, so off we went to Robinson Road to an old cottage at the end of a long winding lane. In the living room, a familiar-looking lady was working away at her laptop. "I think I know her, Misty, but there's something missing."

"Look over there, Fritz, by the front door."

There on a hook, was her hat and it was black. "Misty, your owner was my friend! She helped me write my book, so no wonder you know so much about me!"

Since I didn't know much about Misty, I asked her about her life, and she said: "Well Fritz, I lived in two houses and had many kittens before I was adopted from the SPCA by the lady in the black hat.

Although I used to be very timid, I gradually became quite brave. I even chased a raccoon up a tree once!

We had eight happy years together. Then one stormy day last Fall, I was hit by a car, just like you were Fritz, even though there's hardly any traffic in this very quiet place."

"Then, what, Misty? Were you confused like I was?"

"No, I just

peacefully

floated

away..."

"Okay, Fritz, now it's your turn to choose where we go next."

Off we went to Fort Street and into the kitchen of the house where I was born. After all those years, it was good to be there again!

The same kind lady still lived there, and when she put bowls of food down for her cats, they all came running over.

Two of them skidded to a stop and looked right at me. We gleefully chased each other around, just like in the old days.

Before leaving, I said to my mother and my sister, "I'll be back!" However, I realized that while most animals could see me, not many people could. What a puzzlement...

That was a really great day, thanks to Misty, who had become

my

good

pal.

One afternoon, when I got back from padding about on the golf course, I saw that my little house was no longer on the porch! The front door of the hall was wide open and many people were going in. Lanterns and candles shone brightly on a table by the movie screen.

Flowers and photos of me were there too, and people wrote things down in an open book.

Music played as pictures of me flashed on to the big screen. It was like I was the

star

of

a

movie!

Near the table, my two little houses were on display, along with my food and water dishes. Many people came in and looked at them fondly while they

shared

stories

about

me.

After snacks, everyone sat down and the owner of the cinema got up and talked. He told the audience about how I seemed to know exactly the right laps to jump on during movies. He also said that I was greatly missed.

He introduced a well-known, award-winning author who read his humourous story about me. It had even been broadcast the week before on CBC radio and many thousands of people had heard it!

Then, the lady in the black hat spoke while Misty and I stood beside her. She included the fact that before I had left home to look for the Eiffel tower, I had fathered kittens. She said that if anyone saw cats on the island that looked liked me, they just might be my descendants. I think that means that we'd be related.

She went on to tell how I'd inspired her to write "Fritz the Cinema Cat" for me, and that I'd leapt on her lap during a movie to prompt her to finish it.

She also told the audience that she was going to write a book about me in the "Hereafter".

Then, other people spoke. One of the square-dancers talked about how I would join them and dance in time to the music.

The dog-trainer told about how I'd drive the dogs crazy during their classes and would have to be put outside. The audience laughed and some of them brushed away tears. I jumped from lap to lap, hoping that someone would see me.

A violinist played beautiful music which she'd composed just for the occasion. Then it finally sunk in. This party was for ME! All these people were here because they'd come to say goodbye. It didn't matter so much that they couldn't see me, because we'd always remember each other.

I knew then that it was time for me to go and I said "I'm ready now, Misty."

"Right on, Fritz! Is there anything else that you'd like to do before we leave?"

"Well yes, since you asked. Day after day I sat on my tower and looked across the park. Quite often I had a really strong urge to do something there."

"What was that, Fritz? Did you want to jog around the track or play soccer or baseball?"

"Come on, you'll see." We left the hall and went across to Portlock Park. Then I took a flying leap and landed on the puffy, white tennis bubble that was like a giant trampoline. Misty and I jumped madly up and down and we didn't get the

      least

         bit

            tired!

I took one more look over at the hall, then said to Misty, "Okay, I'm REALLY ready to go now. How do we get there?"

"Well, Fritz, you just have to want to be there, and it will happen. I'll be with you every step of the way. Oh yes, I just remembered something else you should know."

"Oh oh, here it comes. Okay, Misty, what is it?"

"You'll be seeing other animals there."

"What, like crocodiles, tigers and boas?"

"Dogs, Fritz, but they're all really friendly."

"Thanks for the warning, but I can handle them. Anything else?"

"Well, Fritz, in Heaven, we communicate with our thoughts, and that includes people."

"PEOPLE ! Will they be there as well as cats and dogs?"

"Of course, Fritz. We're together here, so why not there?"

"Hmm, that makes sense. And I've always wanted to talk with people." I felt the excitement of an explorer about to discover a new land! I was going to a place more beautiful than I could ever imagine, I couldn't wait!

"Let's

    go

        now!!"

Suddenly, we were there. It was as easy as going from a cinema lobby through a velvet curtain and into a theatre on the other side.

A glowing light surrounded us. "Misty, is it coming from a colossal projector bulb?"

"Oh Fritz, don't you ever stop thinking about movies?"

We laughed, then Misty then told me something very special.

"Fritz, the shimmering white light around us is filled with very powerful love. It's the force of the Universe, and we are all a part of it."

"Oh Misty, is that why I feel so, so... super-ala-splendour-ific-inspir-excell-orious?"

"Did you just say: super, splendourous, terrific, inspiring, excellent and glorious?"

"Oh you're good, Misty, but can you sing it?"

She could, of course, so our happy duet echoed throughout our little part of Heaven on that
          very
              special
                    day...

While I was enjoying my "Fritz bliss", a large group of people appeared. As they came closer, I began to recognize them as islanders who I'd seen at Central Hall!

A man with a short beard and twinkling eyes stepped forward and said, "Welcome dear Fritz! We've been expecting you for quite a while. And it's good to see you again, Misty. You did a great job in getting this obstinate cat over here, by the way."

Everyone cheered Misty. I then recognized the man who had spoken. He used to come to the Cinema quite often with his family. (One of his sons built me my little house! Another one gave me my new name!)

An elegant lady wearing a pink rose, thanked me for keeping her husband company in the cemetery. So she must be the one that he'd asked me to watch over...

Then came the cats and dogs. One dog was small and cute and he said, "Too bad you missed my party! We were due here the same day, but you sure took your time! I was known in the south end of the island as the "Bon Vivant" from Reynold's Road. My owners were a sculptor and a folk singer, and they knew you Fritz. By the way, I'm Dickens."

He then gave us some startling news. "Another island dog is going to be arriving soon. She's seen a gazillion movies, as her owners have the video store in town."

"Oh, they're the people who give away free popcorn aren't they? Isn't there anything we can do?"

"Afraid not. Her time's almost up and there's no changing it. But not to worry, as I'll be there to guide her if she needs any help."

I realized that dogs could be okay, once you got to know them, and I was looking forward to meeting Wilma, the video-store dog.

As Dickens turned, I saw his shiny wings, and I thought,

"How

   cool

      are

         they..."

People told me that they'd seen me at various times at the hall, like on voting day, meetings, and of course, at the movies.

We all walked together until we came to a big wooden building. It had shutters with paintings on them, a peaked roof and a front porch. It was a replica of Central Hall back home. I thought that I was seeing a mirage, which I knew about from desert movies.

Then, I noticed something else. On the porch was a little wooden house with my name over the door.

I sure was

one

happy

cat...

The twinkly-eyed man then asked: "Would you like to see inside the hall, Fritz?"

"I sure would!" We stepped up on the porch and went through the big front door, and they

all

called

out

SURPRISE!!!!

Balloons and streamers floated about, and music began to play. It was a PARTY! That was two in one day. The first one on Salt Spring, was to say goodbye. The second one was to welcome me here. We had a fun time with our friends, and Misty and I nearly danced our paws off.

I was wondering if there ever was a cat that had it so good when someone called out, "It's movie time!"

Misty and I got our popcorn and drinks, and a lady started to play a piano while slides of island scenery flickered on to the screen. Then Misty said, "I hear that it's going to be an old Christmas classic. How will that suit a movie-buff like yourself, Fritz?"

"It's great, as it really does feel like Christmas every day here, doesn't it? Wouldn't it be awesome if it could be that way on Earth, too?"

"Maybe it will, Fritz. Maybe someday it will."

We really loved the show, and near the end of the movie, the family gathered around their Christmas tree. Then, the little girl said: "Every time a bell rings, an

angel

gets

its

wings."

Misty whispered, "It seems that some cats do as well. Look behind you, Fritz."

There, over my shoulder, fluttered a pair of

    really cool,

       feathery,

         white

           wings!

If my island friends could see me now
they'd be looking at a cat with a

really

big

smile!

As the credits rolled, there we were: Misty in her wings and I in mine, and Misty asked, "So where would you like to go to celebrate, Fritz?"

"Well, even though it's great here, there's a certain tower that I'd still like to see.

How

about

PARIS?"

My thanks to everyone
who helped me have
such a wonderful life...

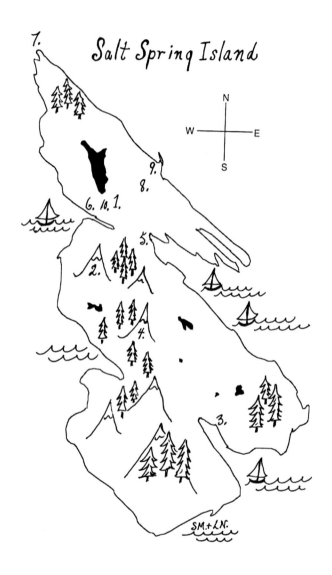

Salt Spring Island

Places on Map

1. Central Hall
2. Mount Erskine
3. Fulford
4. Mount Maxwell
5. Ganges
6. Vesuvius
7. Southey Point
8. Misty's House
9. Fritz's Birthplace
10. Portlock Park

Author

Louise Adela Nye...

Of Maritime descent, Louise was the second of four daughters born to an aspiring-writer mother and a musician father in Toronto. They lived there and in Caledon East with their cat Muffy.

She relocated to Salt Spring Island from Glen Williams, Ont. in 1989 and became an owner of the cinema. Later, she was inspired to write her first book "Fritz the Cinema Cat."

Louise lives on the island and has three children and four grandchildren. Jackson Miles, the youngest (age 7) came up with the title for this sequel, "Fritz the Cinema Cat Gets His Wings." His brother Sam Miles (age 12) did the map outline of Salt Spring Island.

Illustrator

Jo Lundstrom Smith...

Growing up in a large family in Deep Cove, on Vancouver Island, heretofore-unknown illustrator, Jo Lundstrom Smith, has always lived within a stone's throw of salt water, with the exception of an eight-year sojurn in the North Peace River region, (where "the smell of a dug-out could occasionally conjure up the tang of the sea").

Moving to Salt Spring Island in the late 70's to raise her family in a safer and more nurturing environment, this self-described "Luddite" developed her reclusive, somewhat eccentric artistic style, as well as her musical and poetic inclinations.

ISBN 142515193-0

9 781425 151935